BECOMING GOD'S DAUGHTER

A Journey to Discovering
Your Divine Worth

BECOMING GOD'S DAUGHTER

A Journey to Discovering Your Divine Worth

by
Heather Jones

*To those who are broken
who want to feel whole.*

Table of Contents

Forward

Have you ever felt like you were never good enough or had no value or purpose? Have you ever felt so broken that there was no way you could possibly put all the pieces of your life back together?

I promise, you are not alone.

For most of my life, I too lived with these beliefs about myself. Not because anyone told me I was worthless or broken, but because that is what my belief systems told me.

You see, belief systems do not follow rules of truth or fact, but rather rules of emotion and experiences. Belief systems are formed from experiences we have in our lives, whether good and bad, and they influence the way we feel, act, and think about ourselves and others. I love the explanation author Tim Rettig gives about belief systems. He said,

"Your belief system is the invisible force behind your behavior. Together with other factors such as your personality, your genetic set up and your habits, your belief system is one of the strongest forces that affects any decision that you are making. The communication styles you are using. The ways in which you react to anything that happens in your life. Any aspect of your behavior, really...Humans accumulate thousands of beliefs throughout our lifetime, about all aspects of life. We gain them through things that other people say to us, things we hear on the news, things we read, or any other external influences that we are exposed to. All of these beliefs are interacting with one another, affecting one another, and together form a system."

Fortunately, any negative belief systems we have formed throughout our lives do not have to be set in stone. Through hard work, self-awareness, and the grace of God, we can change them!

My hope in writing this book is to show, through my personal experiences, not only how my belief systems were formed, but more importantly, how I changed them and did not let them define who I am as a person today.

I have often felt like the "prodigal daughter" or the black sheep of the family. I definitely paved the way for my younger siblings to look like saints. I have felt inspired to share some very real, very personal, and very vulnerable stories in this book. I will share my deepest secrets and tragedies that I thought I could never come back from. Why? Why would someone be so open about such things?

Because I believe someone out there needs to hear this message. Someone out there needs to know that no matter how lost you may be, no matter how many mistakes you have made, there is nothing you can do that you can't come back from. The love and power of Jesus Christ can and will heal you and put back your broken pieces, stronger than they were before.

I feel passionate about being open with others about the experiences I have had in my life, no matter how dark or uncomfortable they may be. My hope is that these stories will shed light on how important it is to break the cycle of negative beliefs and to help others change their lives through inner healing, and reclaiming their divine worth through the power and grace of Jesus Christ.

So many people suffer in silence and feel like their worth is something that must be earned or acquired. They believe that once it's gone, it's gone. This is a lie that Satan wants you to believe! You are a daughter of God and your worth is infinite and eternal. I want to break the silence for those who don't know where to turn or what to do.

In this book, along with my personal stories, I will share simple, yet powerful processes that helped me to transform my life and change my belief systems. While the stories I share are specific to my life, the lessons I learned are universal. My hope is you will act on the suggestions within each chapter and receive your own divine truths to these specific subjects I will discuss. The Lord is ready to help you, you just must be willing to ask.

"Behold, I stand at the door, and knock: if any man hear my voice, and open the door, I will come in to him, and will sup with him, and he with me." Revelation 3:20

It took me 32 years to learn this process. It has changed my life and helped me discover what was there all along; that I am a daughter of God who is worthy of love, compassion, and forgiveness, and that my value to God never diminishes. NO MATTER WHAT!

If you are reading this book, I believe, it is not by chance. Throughout my life, God has sent specific people to help me along on my journey. I pray that through this book, I can be one of those people for you and that in some small way I can help you see yourself the way God sees you.

Before we begin, I feel strongly that I need to touch on one thing first. Just as I am no longer the same person that I was in my past, neither are the people in my life. The experiences I had were viewed from my perspective, with my feelings and my emotions. This book is about my life, my changes, and my relationship with God.

Some of the stories I am going to share depict parts of my family members during phases of their own life lessons. I value my relationships with my family members and am grateful for the grace we extend to each other as we have grown and changed for the better side by side.

It is my hope that we can always remember that people are on their own journeys of becoming better and we never know what trials they are going through or have gone through. I share these stories with love and compassion and an understanding that we all are seeking to be better than we were yesterday.

CHAPTER 1

Creation of New Beliefs

"For as he thinketh in his heart, so is he:"
Proverbs 23:7

Between the two of us, my sister was the crier. Before she was even spanked, the tears would start flowing. Not me. Like a wild mustang, I refused to be broken. I would try so hard not to cry, but ultimately the pain would be too unbearable, and I could not stop the tears from coming. Many times, after a spanking, my sister and I would pull down our little panties and compared welt marks to see who got it worse.

It was not unheard of for kids growing up in the 80's and 90's to get spanked with the belt, and my sister and I were no different. You see, my dad was raised in a home where, like many of his generation, discipline with a belt was the least of his punishments, so it's no wonder that when he had kids of his own, he disciplined them the only way he knew how. Of course, It didn't help that I could be a mouthy, spit-fire child at times, as well. Since this time, my dad has expressed great remorse and sincere regret for spanking us. He has grown and changed a lot over the years, and I have forgiven him and love him very much.

There was one specific spanking, however, that I will never forget which formed one of the first negative beliefs I had about myself.

Negative Belief: *No one will save me if I am hurting or in trouble.*

I was around five years old and I had done something naughty enough to warrant a spanking from my dad. From my spot on the ground, knelt over the side of my bunk bed, I could see my mom across the hallway getting ready for the evening. As my dad spanked me, I remember crying out to her, "Mommy, please!" I pleaded with her to save me and to make the spanking stop. But she never came; she didn't even look at me.

Finally, when the spanking stopped, I laid there on my bed, silently crying. As the tears stained my pillow, a new belief system was being formed in my mind. I believed that no one would ever come and save me when I was hurting.

Negative Belief: *I am not worth loving.*

Through my tears, I looked up and asked, "Daddy, when is mommy coming home?" There were no words that could shield me from reality. All he could offer was the truth, and so, with pain in his eyes and despair in his voice, he looked down at me and said quietly, "Heather, I have no idea where your mommy is or when she is coming back."

This would not be the first time my mom would leave me. Though my parents loved me and my sister very much, their own relationship and marriage suffered greatly and was broken in a lot of ways. I don't remember exactly when, but eventually my mother did come back home to us. Shortly after she returned, I remember, clear as day, sitting on the bathroom floor watching her brush her hair. My young six-year-old self was filled with emotions too big for such a young child to fully comprehend. I was so happy she was home, yet at the same time, terrified she was going to leave me again. Summoning my courage, I looked up at her and pleaded, "Mommy, please don't ever leave me again!"

I was too young at the time to understand, but now I know that my words broke her heart. She never wanted to hurt me. Calmly and lovingly, she looked me in the eyes and told me how sorry she was for the mistakes she had made and promised she would never leave me again. I believed her, and my little heart took courage in her words. This moment of safety and security was short lived, however, because a few weeks later, she secretly packed her bags and left, leaving nothing but a handwritten letter tucked beneath her pillow.

After realizing she was gone, my dad tried frantically to figure out where she was. Eventually, he found the hidden letter that said she was never coming back and that she felt it would be better for everyone if she disappeared from our lives entirely.

Once more, my dad had to answer the heartbreaking question, "Daddy, when is mommy coming home?" It's hard to describe the feeling I had when my dad looked down at me with tears in his eyes, and said softly, "Heather, your mommy is gone again, and this time, she isn't coming back." Instantly, I felt the weight of a thousand worlds come crashing down upon me. I was crushed and my heart instantly shattered into a million pieces. My little mind could not comprehend why my mom would leave me again.

The next few weeks were some of the hardest of my young life. My four-year-old sister, Shannon, and I would hold each other in our room at night and cry together after our dad had put us to bed. One evening, Shannon was crying in my arms, I whispered a solemn promise in her ear. I promised that I would never leave her and no matter what, we would always have each other. I caressed her beautiful strawberry blonde hair and softly kissed her tiny little forehead. I quietly sang her sweet lullabies of beautiful roses and fairies until she fell asleep in my arms.

At this young age, another belief system was formed. This experience taught me that if my own mother wouldn't even stay for me, then surely, I was not worth loving. It left me with severe emotional damage. Despite having a dad and later a stepmom who loved me and supported me, I often felt very alone. My self-worth as a child was instantly destroyed.

Now, was this true? Was six-year-old me not worth loving? Of course not! Adult me can see that. Adult me knows that she has a loving Savior who is always there for her and that she is worthy of being loved, worthy to fight for and worthy to keep. But at such a young age, I didn't understand that. I couldn't understand that. It was my reality at that time, and it would come to influence many decisions I would make later in my life.

Negative Belief: *No one is going to protect me.*

Suddenly, my dad's world was turned upside down, and he was now a single dad raising two young daughters on his own. Because he obviously still had to work to support us, my sister and I were tossed around between multiple babysitters.
Each morning, my dad would wake us before the sun came out. He would get us dressed and carry us to his small truck that he had started earlier so it would be nice and warm when we got in. He had to drop us off extra early in order to get himself to work on time.
Later in the morning, our babysitters would get us onto the bus and off to school, then watch us again

for a few hours in the afternoon until our dad could come get us after work and we'd do it all over again the next day.

Some of our babysitters were kind, but there was one who, to this day, I have to try not to despise. I have to remind myself that God cannot forgive me of my sins if I don't forgive others of theirs, particularly hers. We will call her Cruella, and she was the last person on earth who should have been a babysitter. I hated going to Cruella's house. She really was that miserable of a person.

She treated my sister and I like servants. We weren't allowed to sit down until we had completed the list of chores she had for us. Some days it was laundry, other days it was dishes or cleaning the bathroom.

One morning as we climbed into my dad's truck to head to Cruella's house, we saw that he had surprised us with a box of our favorite chocolate marshmallow cereal. It was a real treat for us, and we couldn't wait to eat it.

We arrived at Cruella's house and he handed her our precious cereal, kissed us goodbye and headed off to work. Eagerly, my sister and I headed straight for the dining room table, anxious to eat our surprise cereal.

Unfortunately, right as we sat down, Cruella told us we could not eat any of our cereal until we had finished our morning chores. She was the true, living embodiment of the wicked stepmother!

Begrudgingly, but quickly, so we could get back to our cereal, we began our task of tidying up the living room. As we began cleaning, we heard a box being opened and looked to see Cruella pouring two huge bowls: one for herself and one for her son. Happily, her son began gobbling down our precious cereal and I instantly felt rage flood my entire six-year-old body. Watching him eat my special cereal and then ask for more before we had even had any was almost unbearable.

Finally, the living room was clean, and we rushed to the table. As I sat down, Cruella politely placed a bowl in front of me. I looked down to see the tiniest bit of cereal at the bottom of the bowl. Smugly, she said we could have more after school and that she didn't want to feed us too much sugar before we had to leave.

Left to the mercy of this woman, we ate our tiny portion in a few bites and headed off to school. After school that day, we pretty much ran to Cruella's house from the bus stop, greatly anticipating our bowls of cereal we were promised.

We came inside, threw down our backpacks and rushed to the kitchen. My heart sank as I grabbed the coveted box from the counter and found it far lighter than it should have been. I was devastated to learn that Cruella and her son had been snacking on it all day and there was hardly any left. Cruella walked into the kitchen and saw me standing there holding the box. Without a hint of remorse, she told me we couldn't have any until we finished our chores.

That was it! I couldn't take it anymore! I screamed at her at the top of my lungs and made sure she knew exactly what I thought of her and her precious little son.

Before I knew what had happened, she flew across the room and slapped me across the face. She grabbed me and threw me over her shoulder so forcefully, it knocked the wind out of me. She stormed down the hallway to the spare bedroom and violently threw me onto the bed. Scolding me with her finger an inch from my face, she roared that I was not to leave this room and that I was to think about my actions. She slammed the door behind her, shaking the pictures on the wall as she did. I was in complete shock. Too scared to move, I sat there in the darkness for what seemed like hours until my dad came to pick us up.

That evening as we drove home, I poured out my little heart to my dad and finally told him what had been happening. I'm not sure why, but up to this point, I had never told him how Cruella had been treating us. I told him of all the work she would have us do and that she hit me and threw me on the bed. I was desperately seeking validation and acknowledgment from him. I wanted him to protect me, to tell me how sorry he was that that had happened to me. I wanted him to promise me I would never have to go back there, and that Cruella would be punished for how she treated me. Instead, my dad looked over at me and jokingly said, "Well, you probably deserved it!"

I spent the rest of the ride home in silence. My mind was racing, trying to make sense of what had just happened. During that quiet ride home, another belief system was being formed. I believed no one was going to protect me. I was on my own and I was going to have to protect myself from that point on.

Negative Belief: *My worth is based on what others think of me.*

All of these negative belief systems that were created throughout my childhood affected the choices I made throughout my life in some way, but the one that had the most lasting and dangerous effect on me came when I was just eight years old. It impacted the way I viewed myself and made me think that my value only came through how I looked and more importantly, how others viewed me.

Two years after my parent's divorce, I was spending the weekend with my mom at her apartment. I entered her small kitchen and climbed up onto the counter to search the upper cupboards for treats. There were no cookies to be found, and just as I was about to give up and hop down, I saw something tucked snuggly against the back of the highest cupboard. I reached deep inside and retrieved a small zip lock bag that I realized was full of photographs.

Climbing down onto the floor, I was anxious to look at the hidden pictures I had discovered. There was a reason these pictures were tucked far away, not meant to be seen.

Each photograph showed my mom wearing a tiny bikini, posing, flashing, and partying with different men and women. To see my mother in such a violating way destroyed me. As I looked at each photo, I felt embarrassed, and afraid that if I told anyone what I had found that I would get in big trouble.

I quickly put the photos back in their hiding place and tried to forget the whole thing. But it was too late. The images I had seen swirled around in my mind. I began to feel a wide range of emotions. I felt hatred towards the men in the photos and even towards my mom. I felt a deep sadness and anger wash over me and I was overcome with confusion. This would be a hard thing for anyone to process, let alone an eight-year-old girl!

I didn't know how to react, and I certainly didn't know how to feel, but my young mind tried to make sense of it all anyway. Eventually I came to believe that what I saw must have been love.

Suddenly, a deep and distorted seed was planted in my young mind that physical beauty was the most important thing in life. I believed self-esteem was based on other's opinions of you and that your self-worth was determined by what your body looked like and how attractive someone thought you were. I saw how my mom used her body and her outer beauty to gain attention and praise and I eventually began to emulate that.

As I have gotten older and had many long and heart to heart talks with my mom, I have learned that she too battled many negative beliefs throughout her life. At that time in her life, she was broken and lost and was trying to fill her own void. She too lacked any ounce of self-worth or love.

The accumulation of all these experiences at a young age created an internal code or system that I lived by. Each choice I made was strongly influenced by these beliefs. Of course, I had many other beliefs that were instilled in me that were good and positive.

My dad and my stepmom, Linda, worked hard to create a positive, loving, Christ-centered home to raise my sister and I and later, our younger siblings in. They taught me many important truths and tried to counter the negative influences in my life with positivity and self-love.

Unfortunately, many of the negative beliefs I had were so deeply rooted within me at such a young age that despite my parent's efforts, and even sometimes knowing better, myself, I still found myself battling my negative beliefs.

As I got older and became a wife and mother, I could feel my belief systems slowly begin to change. It wasn't until I was 32, however, that I attended a powerful seminar where I learned what belief systems are. I began to understand what mine were and how they impacted my life. More importantly though, I learned that we could change them and do not have to be defined by them!

Now, as an emotionally stable and happy adult, I can look back on these experiences with a new perspective. It has been these experiences that have made my current relationship with the Savior that much more meaningful.

I know that one might read of my experiences and resent my parents and Cruella. After all, I was only a child! To that, I would beg of you to withhold your judgments. You can resent Cruella, sure, but definitely not my parents. Okay, okay, not Cruella either.

Because here is a great truth that I have learned; we are all on our own journey of self-discovery and progression. We ALL need the grace and forgiveness and guidance of our Savior, Jesus Christ. 1 John 1:8 reminds us that, *"If we say that we have no sin, we deceive ourselves, and the truth is not in us."*

My entire childhood wasn't miserable. In fact, much of my childhood was filled with love, imagination, fun, and stability. I understand that at that time in her life, my mother was broken and lost and doing what she thought would bring her happiness. At that time in his life, my dad was young and parented me the only way he knew how. At that time in her life, Cruella was...well, I'm not sure what Cruella was. Clearly, I'm still processing that one.

But I do know that Christ loves her too!

My point is this; just as I am not the same person today as I was in the past because of the grace and power of Jesus Christ, neither are you. Neither is my dad, or my mom, or Cruella! I share these experiences, not to condemn anyone, but to show that beliefs can be formed at a young age and can remain with you and continue to negatively affect you until you change them with the help of your loving Father in Heaven and brother, Jesus Christ.

As extreme as these examples are, not all belief systems are formed by such drastic means. Sometimes they come from seemingly insignificant events. For example, one day, when I was in kindergarten, I remember watching my friend, Sarah. She was wearing a bright yellow sundress and had long gorgeous hair. A boy in our class was sitting next to her brushing his fingers through her hair and told her she was beautiful. I sat there in pure jealous envy, fuming at all the attention she was getting. In my young mind, I believed that I must not be as beautiful as Sarah. That belief that I wasn't beautiful remained with me for years.

Another seemingly small, yet impactful experience happened years later, when I was in junior high. I can remember it as if it were yesterday; I was standing by myself outside for lunch and a girl I knew approached me. I could tell she wanted to say something because she kept looking at my skirt then back up at me. Finally, in a non-threatening way, she asked, "Why do you wear that same skirt to school every day?" Her question caught me off guard. It had never occurred to me that it was "bad" to wear the same skirt to school every day. Looking down at my faded black jean skirt, new feelings of shame and embarrassment began to wash over me. Suddenly, I believed that I must not be good enough, or worthy enough because I didn't wear expensive cool clothes. Her innocent question triggered a new limiting belief system in my mind.

Sometimes beliefs can be as simple as, "I'm not beautiful." Other times, they can be as serious as, "I am not worthy of love." Either way, the influence they have over our lives and our actions is undeniable.

CHAPTER 2

Self-Worth

"Remember the worth of souls is great in the sight of God." D&C 18:10

In 2008 there was a study in a Nation report that showed 75% of teenage girls suffer from low self-esteem. That's nearly 8 out of 10 girls! That study was taken more than 10 years ago, and I can only imagine how much worse it is now. Sadly, I was very much in the 75% during my entire adolescence.

Junior high was a time in my life where I fought with major depression. I had no value in my life or who I was as a person. Adding to my already limiting beliefs about myself was my extreme acne. I hated looking in the mirror at myself because all I saw was a sea of acne. The contorted and disfigured image I had of myself was indescribable and heartbreaking.

I would pray every night that God would take my acne away. I even bargained with Him that if he wouldn't take it away, then to at least move it to another part of my body so I could hide it. I never wanted to leave the house and when I was home, I would just sleep all day and escape my life in my dreams.

My negative self-image and thoughts of not being good enough or beautiful enough consumed me. My acne never got better back then, in fact, it slowly got worse! It wasn't until I discovered makeup at the age of 12 that I began to have a hint of confidence. But makeup just created an outward mask for me to wear, showing the world that I was confident and happy. Deep inside I still had no real value. For the next 10 years, any time I left the house I had to be done up from head to toe. I had to show up with perfect hair, flawless makeup, and wearing the sexiest, trendy clothes to feel like I had any worth at all.

After high school, my skin cleared up just enough to lock-in my new-found confidence. I attended a local community college to play volleyball, and I was like a kid in a candy shop! Suddenly, I was getting a lot of attention from cute football players and guys on campus. It was exhilarating and new. I loved the way it made me feel and it fueled my need to look beautiful and sexy even more.

The volleyball and football teams practiced at the same time, so afterwards, a lot of us would often hang out together. One night, a football player invited us all over to his house for a party. It was the first party I had ever been invited to and I was excited!

This new attention was like a drug to me. I slowly began to act in ways that I knew were not me, but I didn't care. As embarrassing as it is to write this, I started off that night by making out with one of the football players, only to then leave with a different one. This continued over the course of the next few weeks as I attended more parties each weekend.

Before I knew it, I was known on the football team as the tease because I would shamefully make out with a guy and end up in my bra and panties, then unexpectedly have to leave before things progressed to anything more than kissing. When guys wanted to kiss me, I mistakenly thought it was love. I was trying to fill this huge hole in my soul. I was trying to feel wanted and loved and special; something I hadn't felt or allowed myself to feel my entire life, up to that point. Little did I know, that the more I tried to fill this void with false claims of love and affection, the bigger and deeper and darker the hole got.

After a few semesters at the junior college, I decided to move to San Diego with an acquaintance I knew from church. The first few months were pure heaven. I would go to the beach every day and play in the ocean waves for hours. One day on my walk back home, a tall skinny man with a kind face came up and started talking to me. At first, I was annoyed with him, but he was persistent and invited me to come to a party later that night. This is one moment I wish I would have said no and kept walking.

That night I stupidly went to the address he had given me. As I walked in, I felt awkward because I didn't know anyone there. I scanned the room looking for the guy who had invited me but didn't see him. I was about to leave when the most charismatic, beautiful, black man came through the door. He had an energy that drew everyone to him, myself included. He radiated confidence and had a cocky air about him. I decided to stay. A short while later, I was introduced to him. We'll call him Johnny. I didn't know it, but this moment would change my life forever. Johnny was fire in a very bad don't-touch kind of way. But I had to learn that lesson the hard way, I always did.

Johnny and I hit things off from the start. Within a couple of weeks, my life did a 180. All those times I had gotten more and more comfortable with guys was like slowly turning up the heat to boil a frog and ultimately, I did the unthinkable, I lost my virginity to Johnny.

When it happened, I was so numb to the fact that we just had sex that even Johnny joked, "You know we just had sex right?" I should have been more upset, scared even, but I wasn't. I was so empty and trying to fill this void with anything that remotely resembled love.

Honestly, I felt justified because I thought I loved him and that he loved me. In my twisted and broken mind, Johnny was breaking my belief that I wasn't worthy of love. From that point on, he became my whole world, my reason for living. My existence was based solely on his love for me. I learned too late, however, that it wasn't love. Not even close.

Blinded by my infatuation with Jonny, I didn't even hesitate when he told me his lease was up and that he needed my help to get him into a new apartment. Using my name, credit and social security number, I got him and his friend set up in a nice little apartment. Eventually, my own roommates asked me to move out because they could no longer handle the person I was becoming, so I moved in with Johnny.

At this point, it had been a matter of weeks, WEEKS, from the time I first met Johnny to where I was. Within that short time, I had completely lost myself and I started drinking and partying almost every night.

Two months into our relationship, Johnny invited an old friend over to our apartment. I quickly realized she was not just a friend, but rather, a 19-year-old white girl like me, with sandy brown hair and a blue diamond nose ring, and it didn't take long for me to put two and two together and realize that Johnny was seeing this girl and me at the same time.

Instead of kicking him out then and there like a sane person would have done, I vied for his attention and tried to show him why he should want me instead of her by being clingy and needy. Ugh, even writing that makes me cringe. But that was my reality at that time. My self-worth was so entangled with him, I just couldn't let him go.

Eventually, this girl left, only to be replaced by another girl two weeks later. I tried to let it go the first time, but I told Johnny that if he brought her back to our home again, I would fight her. You read that right. I said I would fight HER. I didn't say if she comes back, he's gone. Nope. I was so broken that I was still trying to validate myself to him.

Well, being the kind of person Johnny was, he brought her over again. Surprise, surprise. This time, however, I wasn't going to just lay down and take it. I stood in front of the door and when they approached, I pushed him as hard as I could and hit him in the face. A rage I had never felt before rushed over me. He pushed me back into the house and I punched him as hard as I could. He could see I wasn't going to stop without a fight, so he used his size to his advantage and violently grabbed me and threw me into our room and slammed the door behind him. I screamed for him to let me out, but he wouldn't.

Finally, after a few minutes, he said I could calmly get my stuff and leave because he was going to stay here with his new girlfriend. I couldn't believe what was happening. I had given everything to this man! Still furious, I called the cops. I was not going to let him get away with this!

Unfortunately, the police told me that since I was the one who threw the first punch, Johnny could have me sent to jail. They also told me that since I allowed him to live with me, I would need to give him a 30 day written notice of eviction, and as my tenant, he had the right to invite anyone he wanted into my house.

When the officers asked Johnny if he wanted to press charges, he looked at me smugly and said, "It's okay. You don't have to send her to jail." Even as I write this, I am still shocked at the audacity of the entire situation.

After all of this, you would think that I came to my senses and left this jerk, right? Sadly, I didn't. In fact, I stayed at our apartment and went to bed while Johnny and his "friend" hung out in the living room.

You see, having zero self-worth is a very real and very scary situation to be in because it gives so much control to the other person. Fortunately, or unfortunately, rather, Johnny was a creature of habit, and a short two weeks later, I came home to surprise Johnny one night when he thought I was at my parent's house. Well, the surprise was on me, because I found him and that same girl together, in our bed with nothing on but the blankets.

I'm pretty sure at that moment my spirit left my body I became possessed with a devil because I literally went psycho crazy. All I can remember is screaming at the top of my lungs and my fists were flying, punching him as hard as I could over and over again. My rage couldn't be controlled, and my adrenaline was pumping through my veins and I felt like the hulk. Terrified of my awakened furry, Johnny and his new girlfriend scrambled to grab their clothes and booked it out of the room.

As soon as they were gone, I fell to the floor in the fetal position and wrapped my arms around my body so tightly as if to hold my self together. I began to cry so hard I thought I was going to vomit. At that moment I wanted to disappear and leave this world. The pain I felt was just too much to bear and I didn't want to live.

In despair, I grabbed Johnny's pocketknife and wanted to end it all just to make the pain stop. In one last attempt to find peace, I called my mom in desperation. Through my sobs, I begged her to save me from the pain because it was just too terrible to live anymore. She had no idea what was going on, in fact, no one in my family did. In shame, I had kept my life a complete secret from my entire family. She tried to comfort me as best as she could.

I laid on the floor, silently whispering, pleading for God to kill me, to please just end my life, over and over until I fell asleep from pure exhaustion.
 I was with Johnny for three short months, yet his mark on my life will stay with me for eternity. Like a horrible scar there to remind me of what I went through.

When I woke up the next morning, I packed the few belongings I had and moved it into a friend's garage. She said I could crash on her couch until I found a permanent place to stay. My bruised body was merely a glimpse of how broken I was inside. Desperate to numb the pain, I began drowning my emotions with alcohol and sought for some semblance of self-worth or affection anywhere I could get it. I allowed men to touch me inappropriately and a few I even allowed to be with me intimately.

I was broken in every way. I was a walking shell and was slowly killing myself with no hope or purpose, or any kind of value. I was on a downward spiral fast. The shadow I had become was so dark and all I could feel was misery and despair. I was alone.

Mexico was a short 25 min drive away, and I found myself driving there almost every night. Let's just say guardian angels are real and I shouldn't be alive to tell this story.

I would pick out the most revealing outfits that left nothing to the imagination. I would drive my car into Mexico and find a dark alley far away, stupidly thinking it was better so that no one would mess with my car. I would then proceed to walk by myself to the club to meet my friends. When the night was over, I would stumble back through the dark alley to my car.

I heard a story once about a woman who was walking alone at night. As she approached a group of men ahead of her, she prayed for protection. The next day she ran into someone she knew who had seen her the night before and asked her who the two huge men were walking behind her that night. The woman was stunned but knew in her heart that they were her guardian angels, sent to protect her.

Some may think this is just folklore, but I believe it to be true. In fact, I know I must have had some pretty huge guardian angels watching over me those reckless nights in Mexico. To this day, it gives me chills of my utter stupidity and carelessness. But it also gives me hope that God knew I had a purpose to fulfill in this life and he wouldn't allow my life to be cut short.

It also confirms to me the power of prayer. You see, unbeknownst to me, my dad and my stepmom, Linda, sensed something was not right and had been praying for me every single night and putting my name on the temple prayer roll. This is a list of names that are prayed for by those attending the temple that week.

So, when I say I have a testimony of prayer, I mean it. I know that their prayers literally saved my life and protected me during my trips to Mexico. There isn't a doubt in my mind that their prayers were answered, and my life was preserved.
I knew what I was doing and how I was living my life was wrong. I had been taught better! The thought of disappointing my parents was too much for me to bear, so I avoided them altogether.

Three days had passed since I had talked with them, and my Dad was starting to get worried. He had called several times, but I ignored it each time. After the third day of radio silence, my dad had had enough and set out to find me. I never told him I had moved, so he had no idea where I was or how to find me. But with a little investigating and a lot of heavenly help, he got the address to where I was staying.

I noticed he had called three times within the last hour and had left several voicemails. I listened to my messages and to my complete horror learned that my dad was only minutes away from where I was staying. I was mortified! Not only was I a complete wreck, but the place I was staying at was a party house; liquor bottles filled the shelves and windowsills as decor.

Determined to keep my dad from discovering the truth, I quickly text him an apology for missing his calls and lied that I was at church and my phone was on silent. I had become really good at believable lies.

I threw on some Sunday clothes and a little makeup and put my friend in charge of hiding any evidence of liquor bottles while I ran outside to wait for my dad. When he pulled up, the look on his face when he first saw me is hard to describe. I could see a rush of relief flood over him when he saw me. Alive. I was alive! He had a hard time maintaining his composure. His relief quickly turned to concern as he looked over my thin, frail stature caused by weeks of living on alcohol and depression.

He followed me into the house and to my surprise, my friend had managed to hide every single liquor bottle. I was impressed and thought I was pretty clever to maintain my charade. But even after explaining to my dad that I was just here temporarily until I could find a place of my own, leaving me here alone was out of the question. He pleaded with me to come home. I wish I would have said yes. But in my shame, home was the last place I wanted to be. It took a lot of persuasion on his part, and I eventually left, but only after we made arrangements for me to move in with my grandma.

I had been living with my grandma for a few weeks when I got a call from my friend in San Diego telling me I had left some things at her house. My first thought was to just have her throw it all in the trash so I could completely leave that part of my life behind me. But the curious, broken, and stupid part of me wanted to see what Johnny was up to and this would be the perfect excuse to drop by. So I went.

Believe me, If I could go back in time and smack myself for even thinking this was a good idea, I would have. And then I would have smacked myself again for good measure.

On the drive down to San Diego, I called him and invited him to meet up for lunch as friends. He agreed and we met at IHOP. So romantic, right? As I sat across from him at our table, part of me felt like I had never left. The more he rejected me with his playful banter and teasing, the more I wanted him. I longed for him to tell me how much he missed me and how sorry he was for all the mistakes he had made. I hoped he would tell me that he wanted me back and that he was sorry for hurting me. My hopes were in vain. This was Johnny after all. Those thoughts never even entered his mind.

After lunch, we went for a drive along the

beach. In a horribly twisted, last-ditch effort to get him back and have his love again, we had unprotected sex on the side of some abandoned road. I had hoped it would fill my emptiness, but in the end, not only did I not feel loved, I felt nothing at all. I pushed the emptiness away and clung to the hope that maybe it was enough for us to reconcile and get back together. That hope soon came crashing down on me, however, when I drove him back to his house to hang out. Within fifteen minutes, he called and invited another random girlfriend over and cuddled with her as if I wasn't even there.

At that moment, the reality of my situation hit me like a ton of bricks. Shame washed over me. "What have I done?" I thought to myself. I stood up and before leaving, I told Johnny exactly what I thought of him. I slammed the door behind me and was left alone with my thoughts for the long three-hour car ride home.

The long drive gave me time to process what had just happened and I took a good long look at who I had allowed myself to become. The illusions of love I had for Johnny melted away, and for the first time since meeting him, I could see him for who he truly was. The gravity of what I had done and allowed him to do to me made me feel even more broken and worthless than before.

It is so sad that it took me so many times to learn my lesson. I had been told my whole life, "Gosh dang it, Heather! Don't touch the fire, it will burn you every single time!" But I chose to touch it anyway. This time, however, I was burned so badly I believed I couldn't come back from it. I was crumbled to ashes and wanted to blow away in the wind.

In a moment like this, it may be easy to think, "why would a loving Father in Heaven allow such things to happen? Why would he leave me alone?" Though I couldn't feel it at the time, I have since come to learn that He does not leave us in the ashes. Through the restoring power of His son, Jesus Christ, we can be healed of all mortal burns and be rebuilt, stronger than we were before.

Unfortunately for me though, I still had much farther to fall before I would call upon my Savior for help. The weight of my sins came crashing down on me and I felt as if a millstone was hanging around my neck, ready to pull me down to the depths of hell. I didn't see how God could ever forgive me. Satan had me bound so tightly that I felt no hope. I just couldn't believe that I could be forgiven and have my sins washed clean through the blood of a merciful Savior.

Despite what had just happened with Johnny, and being rescued by my dad, I didn't stop my behaviors. To numb the pain of hopelessness, I continued to drink and party. Eventually, I began to feel something was off with my body. When that feeling didn't go away after a few days, my mind began to race as to when my last period was. When the thought that I might be pregnant crossed my mind, my heart sank. But I had to know. I was absolutely terrified when I took that pregnancy test. I prayed in my mind over and over to please not be pregnant. Yet there it was, clear as day. Staring me in the face was a bright red plus sign. I was pregnant.

How did I let this happen? My whole life I had pictured myself married to a handsome man and having lots of babies and being the perfect stay-at-home mom. This was so far from how I even imagined my life to end up.

The day I discovered I was pregnant was full of every emotion possible. One minute I would be enveloped with pure joy to be carrying such a precious gift. The next minute I would be consumed with the fear of disappointment and shame I knew it could cause my family.

Today, 13 years later, I can testify that this sweet baby girl saved my life. I was on a fast, downward spiral and nothing was going to stop me. Once I found out I was pregnant though, I completely stopped drinking and partying. I got myself to church and instantly changed my focus. My life now had a purpose that was bigger than myself. She was an angel, my own little miracle sent to me in the form of a new baby growing inside of me.

This sweet baby may have saved my life, but I was still fighting a very real battle. I had kept my lifestyle in San Diego a secret from my family because I knew the way I was living went against everything they had taught me and I couldn't bear the shame of what I had done, and I especially didn't want to hurt them. Becoming pregnant was something I just couldn't tell them. So I kept it a secret. It was easy to do at first because I wasn't living at home and I had become quite a good deceiver.

After three months of keeping my secret, however, I couldn't take it anymore and I finally confided in my mom, that I was pregnant. Surprisingly, my confession did not come as a shock to her. She had lived enough of her own life in chaos to know when someone was being deceptive.

She offered me words of comfort and love. I needed to hear those words. But then, her words of comfort turned to hard words of truth that I wasn't ready to hear. She asked me if I was considering placing the child for adoption. Instantly, I was filled with anger. "How can you even ask me to do such a thing?" I snapped at her. I made it very clear that that was not an option and that her advice was unwanted.

Quick to make amends, she acknowledged my feelings and suggested maybe I should talk with her bishop just to see what options are available for single pregnant mothers. Hesitantly, I agreed and met with him the following Sunday.

As a true tender mercy from the Lord, the bishop was so loving and kind. He informed me that no matter what, ultimately the decision was mine to make. He sent me home with a few church videos to watch. The videos were stories from actual birth mothers and single mothers sharing their experiences. Initially, I watched with no intention of placing my child for adoption, but as I listened to these women speak, I had an overwhelming feeling of the spirit rush over me and I knew the decision I had to make. I knew that the precious baby I was carrying was meant to have a life far greater than any I could give her at that time. My heart was heavy, yet I knew that God had a plan for this child, His child, and I needed to place her for adoption.

Once the decision had been made, I felt an overwhelming feeling of peace. From that moment on, I immersed myself in the scriptures and I was in continual prayer with my Heavenly Father. Ironically, though I felt peace and comfort with my decision to place my child for adoption, I was still determined to keep it all a secret from the rest of my family, my dad and stepmom, especially.

I knew I couldn't avoid them forever, so I came up with a plan. Just shy of five months pregnant, I told my family I was going to attend school in Canada and stay with my aunt (my mom's sister) for a semester to see how I liked it.

The day came for me to leave. I said my goodbyes and just as I was about to leave for the airport, my dad lovingly pulled me aside. He took me into the living room, looked me right in the eye and asked, "Heather, are you pregnant?" My entire body froze, and I felt a wave of panic flood over me. After everything, I still couldn't bring myself to tell him. I couldn't bare the shame and disappointment. So, I did what I had gotten really good at doing; I lied. "Of course not, dad," I said playfully. And off I went.

My time in Canada was spent reading the scriptures and relying 100% upon the Lord to carry me through. It was a beautiful and peaceful place of solitude which allowed me to focus completely on doing what was best for my child. My adoption story is one of the greatest, most spiritual experiences of my life, but will have to be saved for another book.

But I do know this, my pregnancy saved me from my own self-destruction and destructive thoughts. I had no time to think about myself. All my energy and all my focus were on preparing to give the best life for her and her future.

I wish I could say that after my extremely difficult, yet sacred experience of placing my daughter for adoption, that my days of trial were over. I wish I could say that I learned all that I was meant to learn, but that simply isn't true. I still had so much learning and growing to do. I just didn't realize it.

Low self-esteem and negative beliefs are not things that fix themselves. During my pregnancy, I focused all my attention on my unborn child and finding the right couple to adopt her.

Through my pregnancy, I had grown closer to my savior and witnessed more miracles than I could count on her behalf, yet I never healed myself from my low self-esteem, and I still suffered from limiting beliefs. Though I was no longer trying to fill my gaping hole with liquor or undeserving men, I still had this huge whole to fix and it wasn't going to fix itself or miraculously. My value as a person was still lacking miserably. More lessons were yet to come. Reflecting on all of this, I have learned that low self-esteem will continue to show up in a vicious cycle of bad decisions until you decide to get to the source of your beliefs and change them. If you don't, you will remain in a constant cycle of self-destruction. I promise you, there is hope! I promise you there is light! I promise you that change is possible through the atoning love of Jesus Christ.

CHAPTER 3

Forgiveness

Come now, and let us reason together, saith the Lord: though your sins be as scarlet, they shall be as white as snow; though they be red like crimson, they shall be as wool." Isaiah 1:18

After I placed my daughter for adoption, I flew back to California to stay with my Mom, Coleen, to recover. To say I was a wreck would be an understatement. I was suffering greatly both physically and mentally. Saying goodbye to my child was one of the hardest things I have ever done in my life. For weeks, I kept myself locked inside. I had no desire to do anything. Despite having just had a very spiritual adoption experience and having felt close to the Savior, deep inside, my negative beliefs lingered in the shadows, waiting for their chance to rear their ugly faces again.

But, over the years, I had become a master at shoving my feelings deep down and moving on as if nothing had happened. So that is what I did. I spent the next few weeks pushing down the hurt, the broken, and the ugly and focused on the good. After all, even though I had limiting beliefs tucked deep inside, I still knew that my Savior loved me. My time in Canada solidified that to me. Though my time there was under heart-wrenching circumstances, it was very sacred to me.

Eventually, I knew it was time to go home to my family. It had been nearly a year since I had seen them, and I missed them terribly. It felt really good to be home! I felt a newness and excitement about my life.

During my time in Canada, I had grown very close to my Savior. I felt his love so strongly for me. I found peace and answers within the scriptures and I wanted to share these feelings and love with others. I wanted to serve a mission. I wanted everyone to know what I had felt and literally wanted to shout from the rooftops that Jesus Christ was our Savior.

I knew, without a doubt that Christ had forgiven me of my past sins. While in Canada, I had worked closely with the branch president in my repentance process. Because I knew I had been forgiven and that we are promised that God will "remember our sins no more," I didn't believe I needed to tell my new Bishop about my adoption experience as I began the process of submitting my mission papers.

As the paperwork process continued, my bishop learned of my adoption placement after speaking with my previous priesthood leader and informed me that, sadly, due to changes in church policy, I would not be able to serve a full-time mission. I was truly devastated. Although I was extremely disappointed, in my heart, I knew that I could still spread the good news of the gospel in my own way.

This still left one problem though. A problem that ended up being a blessing in disguise. When my parents learned that the paperwork process had stopped, they were confused. My dad knew I could not serve a mission, but he did not know the reason. This prompted the inevitable and heartbreaking conversation with my parents that I had placed a child for adoption without their knowledge and what my true purpose was for being in Canada. As you can imagine, this news was a lot to take in and was filled with every range of emotion you would expect.

As hard as it was to open up to my parents, it was very freeing to finally have this weight removed from my conscience. There is a lot more to this story that must be saved for another book, but I am happy to say that today both me and my parents have a beautiful and open relationship with my daughter and get to be a part of her life.

After some time of healing and processing with my parents, I felt it was time for me to move out of my parent's house.

I found a place in Provo Utah and soon my life started to become enjoyable again. But as my life began to be filled with friends and activities, I slowly stopped reading my scriptures and doing those things which kept me close to the Lord. I was working out every day and got my body in better shape than it had ever been and had an awesome tan to match. With my new body came new confidence and of course, new attention. Unfortunately, because I had never learned how to fix my limiting beliefs and I had let my spiritual guard down, I slowly found myself on track to repeat history.

I started serial dating and once again started to fill my self-worth with the attention and perceptions of others. All too quickly old habits returned, and I soon learned that once you are used to going all the way with someone it's a lot harder to set boundaries in the future. I often got myself into situations where it was so hard to stop after kissing sessions. I began to play with fire again, assuring myself I would never mess up again. But that's the problem with playing with fire; eventually, you will get burned.

It had been eight months since I placed my daughter for adoption when I met Russel. He was charming and tall and the life of the party. I should have walked away as soon as I saw him take a shot of liquor, but I was so consumed with his charm and still suffered from low self-esteem that I ignored all the warning signs.

As things go, Russel and I soon became inseparable. Within a few weeks of dating, it became harder and harder for me to stop after just kissing. I'm sure you can guess where this is going. Sure enough, one night I put myself in a place where I was too weak to stop and say no and it happened.

Afterward, I honestly was in shock at how quickly I had allowed myself to give in to temptation and fall into the same trap. Instead of ending things immediately and turning to the Lord for forgiveness, as I should have done. I found my mind flooded with thoughts of hopelessness. I berated myself over and over and thought there was no use to try to repent again, the damage was done, and I may as well not even try to fix it this time.

And in true history-repeating fashion, I again kept my life a complete secret from my family as I continued my relationship with Russel.

Before I go on, there is something I must say. There are many choices I have made in my life that I look back on and though they caused myself and others heartache and immense grief, I wouldn't take back because they shaped me and molded me into the person I am today. But there is one choice I made, however, that I wish with everything I am, to go back in time and erase completely.

It took me months to decide if I was even going to share this part of my life. I had planned to take this sin with me to the grave. It would have been so much easier for me not share it. Thinking about writing it often made me physically ill, especially when I thought about the hurt and disappointment it would cause. But I have received an undeniable prompting from God that I need to share this vulnerable part of my life.

So much of my life has been spent in fear of

what others thought of me. But I no longer fear the judgments of others, now I only fear the Lord. *"He that covereth his sins shall not prosper but whoso confesseth and forsaketh them shall have mercy."* Proverbs 28:13

I do not share my experiences as a confession to the world, but as a hope to shed light that you can overcome your past trials and that there is always hope! Even after the worst of sins have been committed, there is hope. It isn't an easy road to recover from, but it is possible through our savior Jesus Christ. *"Nevertheless, he that repents and does the commandments of the Lord shall be forgiven;"* D&C 1:32)

A mere eight months after I placed my beautiful baby into the arms of her forever family, I found myself pregnant, again. Shock does not even begin to describe what I was feeling. I had just spent nine months of my life preparing to give away my child. How on earth could I possibly do it again? I *couldn't* do it. I couldn't endure the heartache, the emotional turmoil, and soul-wrenching pain of giving up another child.

I wish I had the courage to call my parents or reach out to anyone, for that matter. But the thought of telling my parents I was pregnant again after they just found out that I had placed a baby for adoption was too much. Fear and deep shame consumed me, and I did the unimaginable. I had an abortion.

As I entered the office everyone on staff acted

as if this were as simple as getting your teeth cleaned. Before they began, I told the nurse to let me know exactly how far along I was and that if there was any sign of an embryo already being formed, I was not going to go through with the procedure.

After an ultrasound and an examination, she told me I was very early in my pregnancy and she was shocked that I even tested positive. She assured me that the developing egg wasn't even formed into anything perceivable to the human eye yet and that I was making the best decision. Regrettably, I agreed to the procedure.

When it was over, I could barely comprehend what I had done. How could I have done something so evil and against everything I was ever taught and believed in? I rode home with Russel feeling emptier than I ever had in my entire life. I wanted to crawl into the deepest, darkest pit and stay there forever, but even that would not be dark enough or long enough to hide my shame or wash away the feelings of hate I had for myself.

While I know that my Savior loves me and has forgiven me of this horrendous sin, knowing that I was a part of something so contrary to my beliefs hurts my soul more than anything. If only I had taken the time to really look at my life and the choices I was making and took responsibility for my belief systems and actions in the beginning, things would have been much different. Though I still carry regret for my decision, I was able to forgive myself and no longer carry the shame.

My purpose in being so open and vulnerable with you is this; if you do not make inner healing a priority and find a way to eliminate your negative, limiting beliefs, they will continue to haunt you. You can never push them down deep so deep that they will go away. They will keep coming up again and again. You must allow yourself to heal on the inside and eliminate the beliefs that are hurting you.

My life is a living example of this. I know that my actions and my decisions were my own and I take full responsibility for them. But I also know that the negative, limiting beliefs I held about myself and about others profoundly affected my decisions. They subtly fueled me and silently nudged me my entire life.

My struggles may be different than yours. Maybe you struggle with pornography, drug addiction or eating disorders, depression, or anxiety. Whatever your struggles are, or whatever bad choices you have made because of them, you don't have to allow them to control your life any longer. No matter where you are in your life you can come back from it. The Savior's arms are always open, ready, and waiting to embrace you and bring you back to His fold.

One of my favorite images is of the Savior kneeling next to the harlot in her red dress. Everyone was ready to stone her for her sins, yet the Savior lovingly looked at the woman and told those around her, whoever among you is without sin, let him cast the first stone. The wisdom in Christ's words was profound. One by one they dropped their stones and left the woman alone with her Savior, not one of them having thrown a single stone. It is so important to remember that we all have our own crosses to bear and we must never judge others just because they sin differently than you.

It would be three long years before I would accept responsibility for the way I was living and begin my journey back to the Lord. Three years of lying, deception, and falling deeper into despair. Only a sign from God, Himself, would be strong enough to make me finally leave Russel. And that is exactly what I got.

I moved back in with my parents and I immediately set up an appointment to see the bishop of my local singles congregation. I confessed everything. Every single ugly, heartbreaking, unthinkable sin. I sat there, consumed with disgust for myself and the things I had done. I wished I could literally disappear from the embarrassment and shame of it all. But the thought of dying in my sins and having to face God with the stains of all that I had done was more than I could bear, so I endured the excruciating and extremely humbling task of confession.

When I was done speaking, I sat with my head hung low and braced myself for the worst. I expected judgment and disappointment. I expected shame and reprimanding. I expected anger and disgust. But I didn't receive any of that. Instead, I was met with pure love, kindness, and compassion. My sweet bishop reassured me that I was on the right path and that he was so grateful I came to him. He assured me that my Savior loved me and was there for me. After setting a plan for me to begin my repentance process, I left. I walked away from that meeting overwhelmed with exhaustion. The weight of my sins rested heavily on my heart.

I spent the next year working hard to reconnect with the Lord and allow the power of His atonement to heal my heart. When the day of my final disciplinary action meeting finally arrived, I was overcome with a wide range of emotions. But more than anything, I felt immense gratitude for my Savior. The meeting was amazing, and I felt more love than I had ever experienced.

I left with a heart full of gratitude, yet despite all these powerful, positive feelings, in the back of my mind a subtle voice of doubt whispered, "how can you truly be forgiven of what you have done?" I was fighting an internal battle to allow myself to accept Christ's forgiveness. I found myself in such a strange paradigm. On one hand, I felt immense love from the Savior, but on the other, I still worried that my sins were too serious to truly be forgiven.

The first time I was able to partake of the sacrament again, after a year of being without it, I listened to the sacramental prayer with new ears and a new understanding of God's love for me. The peace I felt in my soul is hard to explain. Once you have lost everything and have been to the depth of hell, there are no words to express how it feels when you are saved from that.

It was the first time in my life I really understood and felt Christ as my literal Savior. He saved me from pain, from turmoil, and from sin. I knew this was true, and I wanted to believe it with all my heart. Yet still, that subtle, silent doubt remained, lurking in the background, constantly telling me that Christ could forgive most of my sins, but my most shameful sin of having an abortion was simply unforgivable.

Christ knew the doubts that lingered in my heart. Not giving up on me, he once again worked through my old bishop to help me. Three months had passed since my final disciplinary council meeting and my bishop called me and asked if we could get together for a follow-up visit to see how I was doing. I agreed and was excited to see him again.

When I arrived in his office, he looked at me with love and compassion and in a very gentle and still voice said, "Heather, I have been thinking about you a lot lately. The spirit has told me several times that I needed to reach out to you. The Lord wants you to know that you are forgiven and to stop the doubts in your mind."

I looked at him stunned speechless! Tears filled my eyes as I poured my face into my hands and sobbed. My bishop continued to talk to me and told me that I had truly been forgiven. He told me that my Savior, Jesus Christ, died for me and paid the price for my sins. Though they were as scarlet red they were washed clean and white as snow. He told me that the Savior knew me personally and did not want me to suffer anymore. The spirit washed over me, and I knew his words were true. It was the first time I felt truly forgiven. *"Behold he who has repented of his sin, the same is forgiven, and I, the Lord, remember them no more."* (D&C 58:42)

Jesus Christ was the only one who could save me from my sins, my sorrow and my inconsolable regret. It was only through Him and his unconditional love that I was able to be forgiven of my sins. Words do not even begin to describe the love and gratitude I have for My savior.

I would soon come to learn, however, that being forgiven of your sins and having a deep personal relationship with the Savior does not free you from future trial and heartache. This experience taught me so much about compassion, forgiveness, and mercy. It is perhaps one of the reasons why I am slow to judge others. Who am I to judge anyone when I have committed the worst of sins and have been forgiven by my loving Savior?

CHAPTER 4

Trails of Faith

"Often we do not know what we can endure until after the trial of our faith." Elder Robert D. Hales

I met my husband, Jeremy during my year-long church probation. Our first date was only a few months after I had broken up with Russel and I was desperate to put my broken pieces back together. There was an instant connection between Jeremy and I, and I knew on our first date that we were going to be married. Right off the bat, the chemistry between the two of us was palpable and very quickly, we found ourselves close to intimacy.

I didn't want to repeat my past sins of immorality, so I did something impulsive and brilliantly stupid. Just shy of two months of dating, I convinced Jeremy that we should get married secretly. I didn't want my family to know that I couldn't go to the temple and I certainly wasn't ready to tell them why.

Getting married after only dating someone for two months is not something I would ever recommend. To maintain appearances, I even remained living at home. Jeremy suffered greatly from the deception. He hated lying to my family about our marriage, but wanting to please me, he kept up the facade. After 5 months of living a lie, the guilt consumed me, and I couldn't take it anymore. I confessed to my family that Jeremy and I had been married.

I was grateful to, once again, have my secret out in the open. Disappointed, but at this point, not surprised, my parents helped us get a place together and Jeremy and I were determined to make our marriage work. Unfortunately, the foundation of our marriage was flawed from the start. We began our marriage based on pure lust and intimacy, but I had convinced myself that it was true love. But we all know that lust does not last and eventually, the honeymoon phase passed.

During this time, I continued with my repentance process with the Lord, but I still struggled greatly with false beliefs and broken ideas of love and relationships. Up to this point I had never been in a healthy relationship and had no idea how to be a wife. I had such a distorted idea of marriage and love that when the lust faded between Jeremy and me, I used intimacy as a tool. I used it as leverage and power over Jeremy. I often used it to get what I wanted or to just be cruel. Because of this, my marriage struggled greatly.

Somehow, we survived our first year and a half of marriage together and I found out I was pregnant with our first child. I knew our marriage was weak, but I had no idea how much my husband was struggling to feel loved by me. My past experiences and trauma with men had taught me to build up walls and detach myself when necessary and I had unintentionally done that again with my own husband. I became cold and hard and I had no desire to be close or intimate with him at all.

Jeremy was hurting. He too was in a marriage that was failing, and he wanted so desperately to feel loved by me. He felt isolated and alone. In an attempt to fill his void, he began casually flirting with female students in his college classes. This was the first small step that lead him to his ultimate infidelity.

Three days after I gave birth to my son, Evan, I found out that Jeremy had been unfaithful to me. I was devastated. Though at times, I had been distant and hurtful towards him, he was the one person I trusted more than anyone and his betrayal broke my heart. Jeremy's actions nearly ended our marriage.

During this time, I felt the spirit testify to me so strongly that just as the Savior forgave me from all my sins, he would forgive Jeremy too. I felt so strongly that I had to forgive him completely to heal and move on. Jesus taught, *"For with what judgment you judge, you shall be judged: and with what measure you mete, it shall be measured to you again."* (Mathew 7:2). These words penetrated my heart and I knew that I needed to forgive him. Honestly, if I had not experienced the type of forgiveness I had with my Savior, I would not have had the strength to forgive Jeremy.

Mercifully, Jeremy's infidelity ended up being a huge and necessary wakeup call for us both. It was a pivotal turning point in our marriage. I knew I didn't want a broken home for myself or for our new son. Jeremy didn't want that either. It took a lot of work and compassion, forgiveness, and humility, but eventually, with the help of our priesthood leader and immense divine strength, we were able to work through it. We both recommitted ourselves to each other and to the Lord and were blessed to be sealed together as an eternal family in the temple a year later.

Through the grace of the Lord, our marriage made it through the storm of infidelity, and we came out stronger than ever. Once again, I thought, surely the worst of our trials were behind us, and once again I was wrong.

We found out I was pregnant with our third child and we were thrilled. We were so excited for our sweet son, Calvin to join his big brother, Evan and big sister, Lily. I was so happy to be pregnant again, yet from the moment I became pregnant, I had a feeling that something was not right. I kept telling myself that everything was fine and that I was just being a paranoid mother. In hindsight, I can see that the Lord was preparing me for what was to come.

At 17 weeks pregnant, the time finally came to have our ultrasound and to find out the gender. The ultrasound confirmed what we already knew, our precious baby was a boy. The ultrasound continued and the nurse didn't say there were any problems with our baby. I was so relieved and knew I must have just been paranoid.

After my appointment, we went out to celebrate and didn't get home till later that night. My phone had died while we were gone and when I plugged it in, I saw that I had a missed call and a voicemail from my doctor. My heart sank into my stomach as I listened to the message which said, "Mrs. Jones, I am calling because I am looking at your son's ultrasound images and there are just a few things I'm concerned about. Something just isn't right. His arms and legs are measuring 2-3 weeks smaller than they should be, and his head is measuring bigger. Please call me back."

By this point, it was 8:00 pm and there was nothing I could do until the following morning. That was the longest night of my life. My mind was racing, and my heart was so heavy, I could barely sleep. The next morning, I was finally able to talk with my doctor on the phone. He told me that he had never seen anything like Calvin's case before and advised me to get an ultrasound done by a specialist.

My appointment with the specialist was scheduled for the next day and we were forced to spend another agonizing night of worry and fear.

The time of my ultrasound finally came, and I laid on the table with Jeremy by my side. I studied the technician's face searching for any hint of answers, but she remained neutral. Kindly, but without any indication of worry, she told me the doctor would be in shortly to review the images with us. 15 minutes later, a female doctor walked into our small exam room.

She sat down and with sadness in her voice informed me that Calvin had a very rare genetic disorder called Thanatophoric Displaysia. She explained that this diagnosis was fatal and that no matter what we did, Calvin would not live. She told us that if he did survive birth, he would only live for a few hours at most. Her words were like a million boulders crushing my soul. I could not hold in my emotions and I burst into tears and sobbed.

She left the room to give us some time to process the news we had just been given. "Why!?" I thought. "How could this be true?" My heart literally shattered into a million pieces. The pain of such news was too much for me to comprehend at that moment. After some time, the doctor came back in and informed me that in cases such as Calvin's, where there is a zero percent chance of the baby surviving, it was legal to abort the baby if I chose to do so.

There was no way in hell I would ever do such a thing again. I told her that I would not be doing anything to this baby and would go full term with this pregnancy.

During the next few months, I cherished every little kick and movement I felt with my son. I knew he was alive. I knew he was my son and I loved him more than I can describe. I pleaded with God to let my son live. I pleaded with Him to find another way. I begged Him to let me keep my son.

Over time, the spirit whispered to me how perfect Calvin was and that his purpose was too big for this earth. I knew God had a plan for my son and that plan was not on this earth. I felt Calvin's spirit so strongly. He was a fighter and I could feel the strength of his spirit so powerfully.

With my new understanding of Calvin's purpose, my prayers turned from asking God to let him live to asking God to let him be born alive so I could say goodbye to him. The remaining months of my pregnancy were precious and sacred to me. My heart was still broken, and I often cried myself to sleep, but I was grateful for that time to celebrate his life, plan his funeral and prepare to say my goodbyes.

As the time approached for me to meet my precious baby, I pleaded with my friends and family to pray that my son would be able to endure the stress that labor and delivery would put on his tiny body and that he would be born alive.

It was a long, slow labor and every effort was made to ensure Calvin was not under any duress. The nurses and staff were informed of the situation and to not try and resuscitate him when he stopped breathing.

The moment came for me to push and before I knew it, my beautiful baby boy came into this world. He let out one loud cry and that was it because his tiny lungs were not developed enough to let him breathe well. I held him in my arms and apologized over and over for not being able to save him. My only concern was that he was not in any pain. I did not want my sweet baby to suffer in his broken body.

I caressed his soft velvety cheeks and kissed his tiny little face. My love for him was overwhelming and my heart ached from the pain of having to say hello and goodbye all at once. I didn't know how much time I would have with him and I tried to memorize every detail I could.

My soul ached, but I knew my prayers had been answered. My son was born alive and I got to spend one sacred hour with him. One hour to hold him, to kiss him and to tell him how much I loved him. During this sacred hour, Jeremy got to hold his son and share his love with him, and my dad gave Calvin a name and a blessing.

The nurse kept checking his heart rate until it had finally stopped. He slowly and peacefully slipped away and returned back to our Heavenly Father in my arms. I held him close and said my last goodbye. We dressed his sweet, tiny body and wrapped him in a soft blanket. A few days later, we laid him to rest until we see him again.

This trial was one I wish I never had to endure. Yet, this experience gave me a purer and deeper faith in Jesus Christ. I became so aware of the plan of salvation. My eternal perspective had dramatically changed. Up to this point, my gratitude for the Savior was because I knew he had saved me, and I had felt his redeeming love. But now, my relationship with him and love for him grew exponentially, because I knew that if it were not for him, I would never be reunited with my son again.

CHAPTER 5

Vision

"Trust in the LORD with all thine heart; and lean not unto thine own understanding. In all thy ways acknowledge him, and he shall direct thy paths."
Proverbs 3:5-6

It has been said, "Greatness starts with a clear vision of the future." No one wants greater things for you than God. He knows you personally, he knows your strengths, your weaknesses, and your potential. He is your Father, and he wants you to dream big! Part of our purpose here on earth is to bless and influence the lives of those around us. If you are not living "all-out", then who else will you be affecting?

As a young adult, I was still trying to figure out what I wanted to do with my life. Without a clear direction, I decided to enroll in cosmetology school. I had always been drawn to hair and makeup, so I thought it would be a good fit.

One evening, myself and 12 other girls from school attended a small event that was hosted by the author of a self-help book called, "The Early Popper." I remember walking into the conference room and seeing this old, short, funny looking man.

He wore a poorly fitted suit and a big smile as he greeted each person who came in. In my youthful arrogance, all I could think was, "What am I possibly going to learn from this old man with fluffy strawberry blonde hair, who obviously needs a better hair and wardrobe stylist?"

Honestly, I can't recall much of what he said to us that night, but before we left, he graciously gifted each of us a signed copy of his book. I said thank you and without a second thought, tossed it into my bag and forgot all about it. I didn't know it at the time, but his small gift would eventually change the course of my life.

You see, when I was younger, I had a serious disregard for authority or anyone who I assumed was trying to have any power over me or anyone else, for that matter. I felt a constant need to stick up for the little guy and ensure justice was served. I became the "Unrighteous Authority Police" and I was not afraid to call anyone out who tried to use and abuse their power. At cosmetology school, this meant standing up to the instructors and, at times, even the director, herself.

The constant need to monitor everyone else's actions and intentions was exhausting. Let's just say school quickly became a hostile environment. Every time I walked through those doors, I felt ready for a fight. I was constantly on the defensive and I could often feel the resentment seething off the staff and even some of the other students because I refused to be silent if I felt like something was unfair.

One day, we had a special guest artist come to teach us. Her class was centered around makeup application and we were all anxious and excited for the class. As the guest artist began teaching, she passed around copies of a makeup book by Kevin Aucion who was a makeover master! I had heard about his book before and desperately wanted to look through it.

The books started on the farthest corner of the room and us girls on the opposite end anxiously waited for our turn. We watched as the books were passed from one student to another. The anticipation was killing me! In the middle of the room sat three of our instructors who sat in on the class as well. When the books got to them, it was obvious that they were in no hurry to pass them on to those of us who were eagerly waiting for them. In fact, they intentionally took the remainder of the class looking through them. They could clearly see how upset we were and would giggle amongst themselves as they slowly turned each page. I couldn't help but feel like they were trying to get back at me for always calling them out.

That was it. My inner defender of justice awoke, and I took it upon myself to see that this would not go unpunished. I rallied my fellow classmates to the cause, and we agreed that after our lunch break, we would all go and speak with the director. As I walked out of class I gave the three instructors a stare that could kill and thought in my head, "You will not get away with this."

I can just imagine what they were thinking as I walked out of the class and straight to the director's door. Speaking loudly so all could hear, I asked to speak with the director in private, informing her that several of the other students would be coming as well after lunch. It was 1 minute till lunch was over and only one other girl showed up to fight by my side. Only one.

I was in complete shock and stood there completely pissed off as it sunk in that no one else was coming. "Really?" I thought, "Where is everyone else?" As mad as I was at the instructors for their behavior, I was more upset with my fellow students for not standing up for themselves. I shared my disgust with the one brave girl who decided to show up and vowed I would never stick up for anyone other than myself, ever again.

In the end I got exactly what I wanted with the instructors. Disciplinary action was taken, the instructors apologized, and I got my justice.

However, I didn't feel satisfied at all. My mind was filled with questions and I felt betrayed by the other girls for not coming together for our cause. I knew something had to change. I took a good hard look at myself and promised that I would no longer fight everyone else's battles, especially if they would not even stand up for themselves.

I went home that day feeling unmotivated and frustrated. I was tired of always feeling called to do something more in my life and always sticking up for the little guy, but always being dragged down in the process. In fact, it usually made me feel even worse.

Still frustrated, but needing something to distract myself with, I dumped the contents of my school bag out onto the table. A good clean-out was way overdue. Piled on the table was a mountain of miscellaneous hairbrushes, foils, trash, and anything else I could shove in there from my locker. I began sorting through the pile when my eye caught hold of a book. It was the book the funny old man with fluffy strawberry blond hair had given me weeks earlier. I picked it up and read the words, "*Early Popper: Secrets of Self-starters.*" I opened it and began to read, the pages still crisp and clean as the day I received it.

I didn't realize it at the time, but this moment, this book, this single act, was one that would start me down a path of self-discovery and self-awareness that I didn't know I was capable of.

Quickly, this book became sacred to me. It transformed the way I viewed the world around me, the way I reacted to others and the way I viewed myself. I learned that I have the power to change, that I have the power to be present and engaged in my life. It gave me a clear vision of what my future could be. This funny man with fully strawberry blonde hair really knew his stuff!

Little by little, as I began implementing the principles of his book into my life, I began to change.

People at school started to notice as well. Within a few weeks, instead of resenting me for being the authority police, people started calling me "Mrs. Heather Jones," because I walked with a different stride. My whole demeanor changed. I was positive, proactive, and no longer involved in everyone's problems. I realized I could still be a defender of justice and stick up for the little guy, but I could do it in a more proactive, nonjudgmental way. I became good friends with the instructors and to this day am great friends with the owners.

So how did one small book impact my life in such a powerful way? Simple. It changed my vision. It changed my vision of myself, of the world and of my potential. My hope is that this book can help change your vision as well. I hope that you can see that change is possible, that your worth, your value, your potential is limitless.

Before my vision shifted, I lived each day just going through the motions. Wake up, go to work, go to school, come home, go to bed and repeat. Most people today live their lives like lemmings. It's kind of like that old computer game from the 90's, where the little "Fraggle Rock" looking creatures follow each other and just keep going in the same direction, never stepping out of line until they fall to their death. This is not the way God intended for us to live our lives! Remember, He is our Father. He wants us to dream big and have joy and meaningful purpose in this life.

It all begins with having a vision. What do you want? What kind of person do you want to be? How do you want to feel? I have found, that when you have a vision, it naturally leads you on a path to discover your personal gifts and talents.

We were not given our talents to be self-serving, but rather to bless and serve others. That funny old man used his gifts to help me along my journey. I, in turn, have used my gifts to help others along theirs. When you have a clear vision of who you are, where you are going, and what your potential is, the Lord will use you to bless others along your way. Your impact for good will radiate far more than you ever thought possible.

The truth is, that funny old man and I are just ordinary people living our lives with a clear vision of what God wants us to be. We are dreaming big for ourselves and God is using us to do big things in our own way.

You are just like us! You have what no one else has. No one else on this entire planet has your experiences, your knowledge, or your abilities. I promise you, there is someone on this earth that needs what you have to offer. So, dream big! I dare you! Don't be afraid to change, don't be afraid to set your vision high and reach for it. Your life is full of purpose and worth. It is there! You just have to look inside and find it.

But here's the thing, vision is merely a dream if you don't take action. I could have read his book and remained the same old Heather. I had to WORK. It took time, and didn't happen overnight, but it did happen! Little by little, my vision of who I wanted to be became my reality.

So, here is what I want you to do. Right now, I want you to take some time and get a clear vision of what it is you want to see happen in your life. Some topics to consider might be personal self-esteem, mental health, family relationships, financial stability, physical wellness, etc.

After you have had some time to think about what your vision is, get a piece of paper and write it down! I love the quote, "If you plan it on paper, God will weld it in steel." Put it somewhere you can see it often, so it remains in the forefront of your mind.

You will be amazed to see that as you focus on your vision, the things you do in your day to day life will change; everything from the books you read, the movies you watch, even the clothes you wear. You will want to surround yourself with people and things that support your goals. It will become evident what isn't helping you on your journey and will, therefore, be easier to let go of.

As a word of warning, I find it important to note that as you begin to make positive changes in your life, Satan will not be happy about it. He is very aware that the changes you are making will bring you happiness and peace and those are the last things he wants for you.

At times, you will find old habits and belief

systems creeping back in. Satan wants you to feel that change is impossible, that your dreams are unattainable, or even worse, that you are not worthy of them. I am here to remind you that you are worthy of them. Change IS possible. Your Father in Heaven wants you to succeed and to dream big! Be patient with yourself as you begin this journey, but most importantly, don't give up. Ever. Remember, you are God's daughter. You are worthy and capable of change, and you are not alone. These next chapters will give you tools to help you eliminate those negative beliefs.

Now it's time to get to work writing your vision. Before you jump to the next chapter, take some time, and write it down. Really do it! Remember, faith without works is dead. You can hope and dream and pray that your life will change, but if you don't take immediate action, nothing will change. Remember, the definition of insanity is doing the same thing over and over and expecting different results. Don't be crazy, okay?

CHAPTER 6

Let God in

"For I am infirm... Wilt thou Grant unto me that I may have strength, that I may suffer with patience these afflictions." (Alma 31:30-31)

Often when we are experiencing a huge trial or feel the weight of the burdens pressing upon us is too much, we wish that God would take them from us entirely. But through the wisdom of His perfect plan and our own agency, this does not always happen.

This does not mean, however, that He is not there for us, or aware of our struggles. Instead, if we turn to Him and seek His guidance and blessings, He will always provide us with the things we need to successfully overcome our challenges.

He does this in many ways. One way is by blessing us with unique spiritual gifts that expand our perspective and enlighten our understanding. He can help change our attitude and provide us with an added measure of patience, comfort, and peace. All of these things help to make our burdens feel lighter and more bearable as we endure them and learn from them.

Often, God does not change the circumstances of our lives, but rather, He changes us from the inside to give us the power and understanding we need to change the circumstances ourselves. For the purposes of this book, I am going to refer to this as inner healing.

When I was thirty-two years old, I was invited to a life-changing seminar. It was at this seminar that I first learned about limiting beliefs and the power they can have over us. During the seminar, we were each given a board of wood, about one foot by one foot in size. We were asked to write on that board one personal negative belief we held about ourselves. I didn't hesitate when I wrote in big black letters, "I have no self-worth".

We were divided into small groups and spent the next 30 minutes focusing on inner healing. We used positive affirmations and allowed ourselves to release our limiting beliefs and replace them with new, positive beliefs. When the 30 minutes was up, the man leading the seminar showed us how to break our boards, symbolizing us breaking our negative beliefs.

When it was my turn to break my board, I stood in the ready position and hit the board as hard as I could. My heart sank as I saw my board still in one piece. I didn't even make a dent. I readied myself again and struck again. Still nothing. Frustrated, I tried one last time and hit it with all my strength. Still, my board remained whole, the words, *"I have no self-worth"* stared me right in the face. Doubt started to flood my mind and I thought, surely my limiting belief was just too powerful to break.

When everyone had their turn at attempting to break their board, we all took our seats. Discouraged, I sat down, my mind still racing with thoughts of failure.

The facilitator asked us all to close our eyes and to raise our hand if we had a breakthrough and were able to break our board. I could feel various people shift around me and a small part of me envied their success. He then asked those of us who were unable to break our boards to raise our hands. Hesitantly, I lifted my hand into the air.

To my surprise, he called me up onto the stage. He asked me to think of a specific time in my life that my limiting belief showed up. As soon as he asked me that, the memory came to me when I was in junior high and was questioned why I wore the same skirt to school every day. It was a seemingly insignificant event, but one that obviously had a lasting impact on me. I shared the story with the audience.

He then asked me to bring someone into that memory to speak with me. It could be anyone, an angel, God, a parent, etc. He told me to have that person tell me the truth about that specific situation. In my mind, I had my mom, Coleen, come into that moment. She expressed to me that the belief I had created about my worth was false. She told me my worth was infinite and I had divine beauty that was not based on my outer appearance.

After my internal conversation with my mom was over, he had me stand on a stool and close my eyes. Then he told me to fall backward. "Yeah, right!" I thought. Sensing my hesitation, he encouraged me to trust him and promised everything would be okay. Trusting his words, I let all my fear go and fell backward into the arms of loving people.

As they caught me, each of them said positive words of love and encouragement. They told me I was God's daughter and that I was amazing. They told me I had infinite value and that I was capable of anything. I felt each word go straight to my heart. With each word, I could feel my new belief being strengthened and fortified. I was worthy. Worthy of love, worthy of kindness, worthy of friendship, worthy of respect, worthy of every good thing I desired. Nothing I could do could diminish the infinite worth I had in God's eyes and now, for the first time in my life, I actually believed it myself.

When I got home that night, I couldn't sleep. My mind was swirling with a powerful sense of self-worth. I felt a newness awaken within me that I had never felt before. My experience at the seminar had opened my eyes and started me on a path to recovery and self-awareness. For the first time in my life, I had the tools I needed to begin my inner-healing journey. I still had a lot of limiting beliefs to let go of and things to work through, but I felt optimistic and knew that change was possible.

After the seminar, I was eager to learn everything I could about inner healing. I had a friend who was blessed with a gift of the spirit to aid others in their own inner healing. I arranged a time for her and I to meet so she could help me work through some other things I was struggling with.

You see, when my son, Calvin, died, I never properly grieved his loss. I feared that being sorrowful and heartbroken meant that I did not have faith in God's plan and that I didn't believe I would see my son again. Without realizing what I was doing, instead of allowing myself to feel the pain and hurt, I buried it all deep inside. For years, I carried this heaviness on my heart, not recognizing the magnitude of the burden I bore.

In my first session with my friend, I could feel the spirit of the Lord so strongly. I felt my Savior's love envelop me, giving me the courage to be completely vulnerable and open as we explored my inner struggles.

During this session, it became clear to me that I was still holding on to so much pain and deep emotions about Calvin's death. My pain was accompanied by immense guilt. I always felt like perhaps I could have done more, tried harder, prayed harder, anything to keep him alive. It was at this time, my friend invited me to visualize having a conversation with my son. In my mind, I talked with him as if I were seeing him face to face. I felt the presence of his spirit so strongly as I talked with him and told him how much I loved him and how truly sorry I was that I could not save him. Calvin reassured me that it was all a part of God's perfect plan and that he had a great work to do. He told me that he was happy and not in pain and that I no longer needed to carry this guilt with me.

Calvin and I finished our "conversation," and my friend and I concluded our session together. I felt a huge wave of relief wash over me and I was overcome with feelings of peace and stillness. During those sacred two hours, I was able to release years of bottled up emotions and feelings. I left my session with renewed joy and literally felt 10 years younger. My session with my friend was not filled with some magical secret knowledge. Rather, it created an opportunity for me in a safe environment to open my heart completely to the spirit and to my Savior.

Inner healing and change are a product of the heart. The scriptures teach us that Christ heals the brokenhearted. If we will allow Him to, He can take our burdens and sorrows from us and heal us. But we must be the ones to give them to him. Yes, there are times in our lives when Christ will lighten our load and give us the strength to endure our trials. I am not talking about those trials, I'm talking about the soul-wrenching, heartbreaking struggles we carry deep inside, the pain, the hurt, the self-doubt, the self-loathing, etc. Those are the things that we do not need to hold on to! Often, we are the culprits of our own sorrow because we refuse to release it and give it to our Savior who is waiting and wanting to take it from us.

Sometimes, like with my son Calvin, we don't even realize we are clinging so tightly to it. Other times, we wear our self-loathing like a badge of dishonor, a constant reminder of our faults and lack of worth.

The good news is, we are not doomed to carry the weight of our struggles forever. There is a way to completely shake off the chains Satan has put on our hearts and minds. This freedom comes through Jesus Christ. If we give our whole selves to Him; our hearts, our pains, our burdens, our joy, our everything, he will help us.

It is important to understand that sometimes our burdens are taken immediately, while other times he may seem slow to listen. But I promise whatever he chooses to do is for our maximum learning and benefit. Elder Richard G. Scott who is a leader of the Church of Jesus Christ of Latter Day Saints explains that God loves us perfectly and "would not require us to experience a moment more of difficulty than is absolutely needed for our personal benefit or for that of those we love."

When we understand that God's intentions are to help us and not punish us, rather than being mad at Him, we can actively look for what it is he is trying to teach us.

One way we can do this is by creating

opportunities for us to hear and feel the spirit. We are often taught to be still and listen. Seek God's will for you. When you pray, instead of asking God for a cure or to take away your problem, ask him also to teach you and give you guidance. Ask Him, "What is the lesson I need to learn and where should I go from here?"

I encourage you to find a quiet space where you can sit and ponder. Be open and honest with yourself as you look at the patterns that keep showing up in your life, whether they are good or not-so-good. When a negative belief or habit that does not serve you becomes evident, ask the Lord if you need to explore it further. If you feel there is more that you need to understand about it, sit in stillness with the spirit until impressions come to you on what you need to learn, what you can do or change or any other specific instructions you may receive from the Lord.

If you don't feel the need to understand more about a particular negative belief, then it is time to release it. You do this by breathing in and imagining the light of Christ filling your entire body. As you exhale, release the negative belief, and give it to Christ.

Each day, check-in with yourself and with the Lord. We must remember that our life's progress is not measured by what we are doing but who we are becoming. Some days you may feel discouraged or like you can't do it on your own. Don't forget that "with man this is impossible, but with God all things are possible." (Mathew 19:26) When you are in alignment with God you will be at peace. Christ has promised, "peace I leave with you, my peace I give unto you: not as the world giveth, give I unto you. Let not your heart be troubled, neither let it be afraid" (John 14:27)

As we turn to Christ and choose to let go of the things that no longer serve us, we will live each day with purpose and focus. We then stop living in the past and worrying about the future we will live fully in the present and what God would have us learn, do and be in each moment. The act of being present is one of the greatest tools for inner healing.

I love the scripture in Mathew 6:31-34 that says, "Therefore do not be anxious, saying, 'What shall we eat?' or 'What shall we drink?' or 'What shall we wear?' For the Gentiles seek after all these things, and your heavenly Father knows that you need them all. But seek first the kingdom of God and his righteousness, and all these things will be added to you. Therefore, do not be anxious about tomorrow, for tomorrow will be anxious for itself. Sufficient for the day is its own trouble."

As you will learn in the next chapter, when you start your day off right with your morning routine which includes being still and listening, you create the intention for your day. This will help you to be an active representative of your life. Rather than allowing the situations that arise to dictate your destination, you will be the commander of your ship and your course will be set to where God would have you go.

Having this direction and understanding each day allows you to ask what the Lord would have you learn when an obstacle arises. Focus more on the lesson you need to learn and worry less about the problem. Choose to see everything as an opportunity to grow and a lesson to become more Christ-like. Remember, this doesn't happen overnight. Yes, you can release limiting beliefs, but you are still human and often, it will take constant, consistent and repetitive work each day to find lasting changes.

CHAPTER 7

Building a Solid Foundation

"Therefore, everyone who hears these words of mine and puts them into practice is like a wise man who built his house on the rock." Mathew 7:24

In my search for self-improvement, I have read countless books and attended numerous seminars. Through all my learning I have found one common theme among successful, happy individuals; They all have a specific morning routine. So, not wanting to recreate the wheel, I gave it a try. And you know what I discovered? They are right! I learned that how you start your morning will determine how successful you will become. Not if, but when.

I read a quote once that said, "Every morning you have two choices; you can either continue to sleep with your dreams or wake up and chase them." The morning is the start of a brand-new day and a new you. You get to decide what kind of day it is going to be because your morning sets the expectations for the rest of your day.

Each morning, I take one hour to complete five

things that help me have a productive, happy, and successful day. Some people refer to this as their Hour of Power. I promise, that if you will take the time each morning to implement these 5 things, you too will experience positive changes in your day to day life. Keep in mind that these do not have to be done in a particular order. Always do what works best for you.

Prayer

When you begin your day with a conversation with Father in Heaven, you are showing him that you are open to, and wanting his guidance and direction. In the morning when you rise and offer your prayers to God in the name of Christ, you offer yourself. You are not just asking for things but more importantly, you are committing yourself to Christ's things.
You are asking Him to guide and direct you through your day.

Your morning prayer is the foundation upon which you are building the rest of your day. Remember the wise man who built his house upon the rock? Well, when the rains came down and the floods came up, his house didn't budge! And we all know what happened to the foolish man's house! Life is going to throw major obstacles your way. Each day will provide different challenges and trials, but when you start each day with God on your side, He will help guide you through.

Meditation

This is a time to find a nice quiet space free from all distractions. Make sure your phone is turned off or better yet in a different room. Allow this time to completely free your mind and be in a space of gratitude. If you choose, you can listen to calming meditative music. You can even do a guided meditation.

During this time, be completely in the present. You cannot control the past or the future, you can only control how you live today.

Kara Brandt created these mantras for her morning meditations to start the day off right and to help her focus on the present.

"Just for today, I choose kindness. Just for today, I choose patience. Just for today, I choose humility. I choose to be honest with myself and others. I give thanks for all that comes into my path, for each is my teacher. Just for today I will have compassion and show unconditional love to all I meet. Just for today, I choose love. Just for today, I choose light."

Exercise

This can be anything that gets your heart pumping. I personally love to use my mini rebounder trampoline for 20 min. You can dance, run outside, do yoga, go on a hike, whatever your heart desires. Of course, 20 minutes is just a minimum amount of time. You can work-out much longer. It's all up to you.

Journaling

For 10 minutes, without stopping, write whatever comes to your mind. There doesn't have to be any rhyme or reason to it. Just make sure to keep writing. It's amazing what ideas and thoughts come to you when you write freely, without thinking too hard about it.

Read

Spend 10 minutes each morning reading any non-fiction book. This can also be your scriptures. This does not, however, include audiobooks. Those are great, but this time is specific to actual reading. I suggest having a highlighter and pen for anything that stands out to you or to write down inspiration that comes to you.

To this day the most important thing I can do for myself and my family is starting my day on the right track. One hour might not seem like a lot of time to change your life, but over the course of a week, a month, and a year, it adds up.

It is the small and simple things we do daily that makes the biggest impact on our lives. No one wakes up one day with washboard abs or with a mastered skill. It all takes time. Nothing worth fighting for ever came easy. If that were the case, then everyone would be able to do open-heart surgery or fly a plane or even better, shuttle to the moon.

This morning routine will keep you in

alignment with accomplishing your goals and your vision. When you prepare yourself in the morning it's like preparing yourself for battle. With God's direction each morning, you are literally putting on his armor to get you through that day and strengthening your foundation for days to follow.

I have found that when I wake and follow these steps I accomplish more and am a better mother, wife, friend, and daughter. I put myself in a more present and focused mindset. When I don't do these steps, I find myself unorganized. I waste valuable time and worry about things I cannot control.

For example, after graduating from cosmetology school, I set the goal to build my own in-home salon. Although I had an initial vision of what I wanted my salon to look like, at this time in my life, I didn't know anything about an hour of power. I woke up each day, unsure of what I was going to accomplish. I knew I wanted to get things done, but I lacked focus and didn't have a plan. Some days I wasted so much time stressing over all the things that needed to get done that I ended up not doing anything.

Eventually, after a whole lot of blood, sweat, tears, and stress, it got done and it was beautiful! I look back at that time and think of how much better it would have been had I been implementing an hour of power in my life. Instead of waking up each day on a whim, I would have had my vision in mind and set myself up each morning for success. I would have been prepared; mentally, physically, emotionally, and spiritually to take on what needed to be done to accomplish my goal of completing my salon.

Sure, it still would have required sacrifice on my part and most likely still would have included some blood, sweat, and tears, but I am certain it would have taken less time and been less emotionally draining. My days would have been established on a strong foundation and would have been happier and more productive.

Tiffany Peterson, a female entrepreneur I admire, said something that hit me hard. She said, "Whatever you water in your life will grow. The same thing goes for whatever you don't water. It will die." Meaning, whatever you are "watering" aka, spending your time and energy on, it will grow. This can either be a good thing or a bad thing.

What are some things that are dying in your life? Is it your health? Your relationships? Your finances? I looked more closely at where I was focusing my time, and what "plants" I was watering. I realized that I was giving a whole lot of water to my Facebook and Instagram plants. So much so, that it left me no time at all to water my relationship plants which were slowly withering away. I was spending more time on my social media accounts than I was spending with my own husband! This was a huge wakeup call for me.

Your hour of power each morning will help you become more aware of what you are watering in your life and if it is helping or hindering you from reaching your goals.

As you devote an hour each morning to connect with God and seek his guidance, to fill your bucket, and to prepare yourself mentally, physically and spiritually, it will become clear to you what weeds need to be pulled from your life. Not only will it become clear what needs to go, but you will also have greater determination and power to get rid of it and let it go. I challenge you to make the decision right now to focus on what needs more nurturing and watering in your life and watch it grow into something beautiful.

"Daring to set personal boundaries is about having the courage to love yourself even when you risk disappointing others."

It took me 30 years to really see boundaries as a protection of mind, body, and spirit. Ultimately, you are responsible for what you will and will not allow into your life. Having healthy boundaries, shows yourself and others that you respect yourself enough to say no and that you recognize your value and worth. Honestly, this is something I am still working on. Because I like to please people, it is easy for me to be a 'yes' woman. Often, I would take on more than I could handle and my relationships that mattered most, those with my children and husband would suffer because I had nothing left for them at the end of the day.

I had to learn that it is okay to say no. It's okay to say no to friends who were taking advantage of my talents and skills, it's okay to say no to family in order to have more time with my children, it's okay to say no to work opportunities that don't align with my values.

Initially those in your life who mistreat, take advantage of, manipulate, or are unkind to you, will struggle with your new boundaries because they will expect your relationship to be as it always has been. But as you continue to hold tight to what you want and need, they will either fade out of your life, or they will begin to treat you as you wish to be treated. When you recognize your worth and understand your purpose in life, it is easier to cling to your boundaries.

Yes, there are people in this world who will jump at every opportunity to take from or abuse you. But many times, people are not aware of the fact that they are even doing so. Sometimes we don't even recognize toxic relationship patterns ourselves. Once we do, however, the responsibility falls upon us to make and set healthy boundaries. This is not always an easy thing to do. It can be hard to step back and view your life and relationships in a new light. It can be scary to set boundaries for fear of what or who you might lose. But you will soon find that the things you gain will far outweigh that which you lose.

When my husband and I first got married,

validation from my dad was incredibly important to me. Because of this, his opinion and input weighed heavily on my decisions and I often allowed him to dictate certain parts of my life. It was not malicious on his part. We both had just been so accustomed to the way our relationship worked and the roles we each played. During this time, I said yes to everything that was asked of me and eventually it started to cause tension and resentment between my husband and I.

When it was brought to my attention and I was able to look outside of my situation and see it with new eyes, I saw clearly that some things needed to change and some healthy boundaries needed to be established; boundaries that allowed me to fulfill my new role as wife and mother, while still maintaining a healthy role as daughter.

Another, more extreme lesson on setting boundaries came recently with a close friend whom we will call, Rose. Rose was a fun, feisty, no-nonsense, say-it-how-it-is, kind of friend. At first our friendship was wonderful. Eventually, though, things began to shift, and it became evident that I needed to distance myself from her a little bit, or at least set stronger boundaries. You see, Rose and I worked various events together and she began to ask me to do things that I didn't feel comfortable doing. But because I was afraid of confrontation and still wanted to please her, I allowed things to continue as they were.

Eventually, we even started a business together. As our business got off the ground, it had been six months and I still had not been paid my share. Each time I asked her about it she had one excuse or another. I kept my frustration inside and never voiced my concerns about various aspects of our relationship.

Ultimately, it took her screaming at me in front of a group of people at an event for me to finally get the courage to end our friendship. It should have happened years before, but I had never set boundaries and never stood up for myself, or had the courage to say no. Had I learned earlier to set boundaries and say no, maybe she and I would still be friends. Maybe then, she would not have felt free to take advantage of me.

It is not just mental and emotional boundaries that need to be set either. It is essential that we set firm, undeniable physical boundaries as well. This is a lesson I wish I had learned and mastered when I was young. I would have saved me a great deal of heartache and shame.

For example, one time when I was a young adult, I met a guy at a party. He took me upstairs to a room full of his friends and lifted my skirt to show everyone how fine my butt was. I cringe even typing that! I should have slapped him right then and there! I should have told him he was a creep and stormed out of the room! But I didn't even stop him.

I wish I had known sooner that I was in control

of what I allowed into my life. I didn't know that we literally teach people how to treat us by how we allow them to act in our presence. We are the creators of the world and environment around us. We get to decide what we will and will not accept into our realm of existence.

Take the Queen of England, for example. Do you think for one second that people step out of line around her or treat her with even a hint of disrespect? I don't think so! Her boundaries are clear and understood by all. We should all take a lesson from Her Majesty on this one.

Be the Queen of your life! Of course, that doesn't mean be rude or look down upon others, but remember that you are quite literally God's daughter, a princess in your own right! You deserve to be treated as such. The more you come to learn of your divine worth and how truly special and important you are to your Savior, your self-esteem will blossom and you will see more clearly the importance of setting strong, healthy boundaries.

This should be your expectation, not your hope. Your life doesn't have to suffer because someone else wants to pull you down, treat you badly, or take advantage of you. If they don't fit the bill, send them on their way. Free yourself of that toxic relationship and move on with joy and happiness. By doing this, you are setting yourself up for success and not settling for anything less.

CHAPTER 8

Inner Healing

"Peace I leave with you, my peace I give unto you: not as the world giveth, give I unto you. Let not your heart be troubled, neither let it be afraid."
(John 14:27)

True inner healing requires repentance and a desire to change. Inner healing is a product of the heart when we arrived at an inner conclusion and commitment to follow Christ. It does not require magic or a deep knowledge and understanding of gospel principals to come to learn how to heal yourself from the limiting beliefs created over the course of your life.

Often, people will grow up never learning the truth that they do not have to carry these burdens alone or even at all. There is a way to change completely and shake off the chains Satan has put on our hearts and minds and be free. "Awake, awake; put on thy strength, O Zion! Shake thyself from the dust; arise and sit down, O Jerusalem: loose thyself from the bands of thy neck, O captive daughter of Zion."

Healing Involves a spiritual and emotional intertwining of our life story. Not only must we go back in time to correct and remove limiting beliefs, but we must learn how to change and move forward. This involves growth, personal change, and maturity to transform into a new state of deeper trust in God even during times of adversity.

Personal revelation is a gift and a power we can use for our own self-healing. All we need to do is go inside and listen for the answers.

We are taught to be still and listen to the still small voice. If true inner healing is wholeness, a oneness with God in mind body and spirit, then healing can take place only as we obey the Scriptures to *"be still and know that he is God."* (Psalms 46:10) It is essential that we learn to be quiet and to listen to his spirit. When you pray, instead of asking God for a cure ask him also to teach you and give you guidance.

What is the lesson you needed to learn and where should you go from here? We must remember that our life's progress is not measured by what we are doing, but *who* we are becoming. It is so hard for us to try and do things by ourselves. Most days I often wondered if it was even possible at all. The answer is that *"with man this is impossible; but with God all things are possible."* (Mathew 19:26)

I encourage you to find a quiet space where you can sit and ponder and really look at the patterns that keep showing up in your life for the good and for the bad. Inner healing comes to us through Gods spiritual gifts such as the Holy Ghost. We are given answers from within and when we ask, we shall receive. Once you have found a few beliefs that keep showing up in a negative way that don't serve you, ask yourself if you need to know more about this belief. If you do not, choose to release it by simply breathing in and imagining the light of Christ feeling your entire body and then exhale the limiting belief that no longer serves you. If inside you felt that you did need to know more, sit with that until the impressions come to you on what it is you need to learn.

Another word that could be used to describe inner healing is wholeness. Wholeness is the combination of body, mind, spirit, and God. When you are in alignment with God, you will be at peace.

Often, I would look for healing and comfort and love in other ways which always left me in more despair then before, yet Christ can and always will give us the wholeness we are so desperately seeking. The Lord asked "*will ye not now return unto me, and repent of your sins, and be converted, that I may heal you?*" (3 Nephi 9:13)

I am no longer the person I was 10 years ago when I first met my husband, and I continue to learn and grow. We can choose to stay stuck in the cycles of limiting beliefs, or we can choose today to no longer allow damaging beliefs to constrict us.

When we choose to let go of the things that no longer serve us, we can then live each day with purpose and focus. We then stop living in the past and worrying about the future and be more present in the now. Our eyes can be awake to the truth and to our true reality that we are eternal beings with infinite divine worth.

We can each be influenced today through the healing power of Christ especially understanding his healing as wholeness. We should strive to seek our Saviors healing, not only during times of trials or sickness and physical health, but for our souls as well. We need to let our Savior's love and mercy come upon us and teach us what he would have us learn and feel from our present situation and what he would have us do.

Our savior will help us align our hearts with God and give us peace. He will help make us whole. This type of healing allows Christ divinity into a broader spectrum of our daily infirmities which includes not just mere physical health but the healing of our minds, emotions, hearts, and spirits as well as our limiting beliefs.

The act of being present is one of the greatest tools towards inner healing
Mathew 6:31-34 "Therefore, do not be anxious, saying, 'What shall we eat?' or 'What shall we drink?' or 'What shall we wear?' For the Gentiles seek after all these things, and your heavenly Father knows that you need them all. But seek first the kingdom of God and his righteousness, and all these things will be added to you. Therefore, do not be anxious about tomorrow, for tomorrow will be anxious for itself. Sufficient for the day is its own

trouble."

Living in the present will lead to a more full and happier life of purpose. When you start your day off right with your morning routine you create an intention for your day, and this will help you to be more aware and be an active representative of your life. You will be the commander of your ship. You will be fully awake and able to make the best decisions for yourself.

Before I knew these steps, I would often wake up each day and just go through the motions of life. I was never really present. It was almost as if I was having an out of body experiences and allowing whatever came into my life to have control over it. Now that I am fully present, I can look at the situations or obstacles in my life and ask myself, what is the lesson I need to learn from this situation?

Everything that happens in our life is for a reason and is meant to help us grow. Focus more on the lesson you need to learn and worry less about the problem. We always have the choice to choose to see life in a positive or negative outlook and it all comes down to our perspective. Choose to see everything as an opportunity to grow and a lesson for us to become more Christ like. When you do this and try to live fully present, your life will change drastically

How does a plane of such gravity and weight get off the ground? It takes resistance. If there is no resistance, a plane cannot take off. When we are trying to change our lives and take off just remember resistance will come and it's the necessary law for takeoff. If you are in the storm right now in your life lean into it, resistance is key.

How do you know when you are on track to change your life? Well it's quite simple actually. The more you try to become like Christ, the more Satan will do everything in his power to stop you.

Life is a classroom and the same lessons will repeat until you learn what is needed to move forward. The lessons in my life were so hard and almost unbearable to overcome and as you saw I made the same mistakes repeatedly in my life. Each time I thought I would never commit the same sin again and yet I failed every time. It wasn't until I awoke and became fully aware of my actions and limiting beliefs and stopped putting the blame on anyone else. I stopped seeking validation and worth from others. I started to fully see my life and put things into perspective instead of just going through the motions and allowing whatever to come my way and hurt me.

I was able to take a step back and look at what I was believing to be true in that moment and checking in to see if that was serving me or not. If there was something I needed to learn, I would allow myself to feel the emotions and be present. I would then end with choosing into the new belief and shift into a more positive outlook, which ultimately stopped any reoccurring cycles from showing back up

Elder D Todd Christofferson said, *"You may ask, why doesn't this mighty change happen more quickly with me? For most of us, the changes are more gradual and occur over time. Being born again, unlike our physical birth, is more a process than an event."*

Transformation is a spiritual gift from God, not an accomplishment earned by our efforts. It causes us to be humble seekers and receivers, not prideful earners and accomplishers.

George Q Cannon taught: "If any of us are imperfect, it is our duty to pray for the gift that will make us perfect. Have I imperfections? I am full of them. What is my duty? To pray to God to give me the gifts that will correct these imperfections. If I am an angry man, it is my duty to pray for charity, which suffer long and is kind. Am I an envious man? It is my duty to seek for charity, which enviteth not. So with all the gifts of the gospel. They are intended for this purpose. No man ought to say, 'oh, I cannot help this; it is my nature.' He is not justified in it, for the reason that God has promised to give strength to correct these things, and to give gifts that will eradicate them."

You have to enjoy the journey of life. I am a mother of 3 small children and another on the way. Let me tell you, the journey isn't always pretty, and it can still be extremely hard. I have to remind myself to stop and enjoy these moments of my sweet children. They won't be little forever and someday they won't beg and plead for my attention 24/7. Life is all about the little things. Small things on a daily basis make the biggest difference in our lives.

Sometimes we see the journey of our lives and get overwhelmed. The worst situation the devil can imagine is a soul who is firmly planted in the present moment. All unhappiness (when there is no immediate cause for sorrow) comes from excessive concentration on the past or from extreme preoccupation with the future.

CHAPTER 9

Testimony

How can I put into words the love I have for every person reading about my journey knowing each of you have had your own trials and crosses to bare? How can I express truly what it means to be born again of the spirit and flesh and to know your worth and value as a child of God? I personally want to reach out to you and hold you and pray over you and show you how amazing and priceless you are in Gods eyes. My heart's desire is for you to feel Gods infinite love for you no matter how tattered or torn or broken you may think or feel you are.

It is true and I testify that God loves each and every one of us and knows us personally. You are Gods daughter. We lived with him before we came to this earth and have been prepared to come at this specific time. I pray that this book gives you hope and the tools you need to start changing your life today. I must warn you however that the healing process as I have said before is a journey and it takes daily time and practice. Healing does not mean we forget what has happened to us or what we have done, but healing comes knowing that through our savior Jesus Christ we can and will be healed and made whole.

Our wounds will be healed but the scars are left as reminders of where we have come from and what we have overcome. We are all here to make it back to our Heavenly Father and no one comes back unscathed from the world. Every trial we have gone through is a lesson that we can learn and grow from.

One might ask what one can learn from the most wicked offenses, but I say to you compassion for those who have travelled in your shoes. My trials have been hard to bare at times but I would not take away one because of the compassion humility and Christ like Love I now have for my brothers and sisters. Tragic things happen every day and life can be so unfair, but god has promised to make up the difference and make everything right.

To end, I leave you with a blessing and a prayer. I humbly pray and ask in the name of Jesus Christ to bless the lives of all those who read this book that they may know how much you love them individually and personally. I pray that I may be used as an instrument in your hands to be a help meet unto your children. I pray and ask that you will shower your love and mercy upon them and that the powers of heaven will pour down upon them to heal and renew their bodies. I pray that you will have the courage and strength to be able to change your life from this day forward and be born again through the power of the Holy Spirit. I pray that you will seek gods help and council and that you will be made whole again through the atonement of our savior Jesus Christ. I pray dear god that your spirit will be them.

A Free Gift to you:

As a thank you for investing in yourself and taking action immediately, I want to gift you a free 30 min coaching session to help you jump start your journey to change your life (www.todaysheis.com)

In addition, join my private Facebook Group (@todaysheislimitless) which will give you access to a community of likeminded people who want to change their lives and make a difference in the world.

You can also follow my podcast to dive deeper into the different healing modalities with guest speakers from diverse backgrounds and much more....
You can find me on Apple Podcasts and Anchor Podcasts @Heather Ashley Jones.

If you are like me and don't want to change just one area of your life but want to change your **ENTIRE LIFE,** jump all in and join my exclusive tribe, *Gods Daughters* to learn the Ultimate Healing Tools through my private group program. Visit www.todaysheis.com for more info.

Acknowledgments

This book would not be what it is today without the countless hours my sister Shannon spent transforming my words into a clear and beautiful story. My sister has been by myside through my entire life and I am so blessed. Shannon no words can describe the love and bond I have for you. You've been a light through my darkest hours, a strength when I had none, and a voice of assurance during uncertainty. When God sent you to this earth an everlasting bond was created and for that I will forever be grateful. I hope seeing this book published gives you as much joy and accomplishment as it does me. This truly was a combined effort, thank you for this priceless gift, your endless support, influence, and love.

My adoring husband Jeremy, thank you for watching our wild kids so I could work on my book and encouraging me to leave the house so I could write in a quite environment. You have always supported me in all my adventures even when that meant writing a book that exposed some of our hardest trials. This past decade has been full of growth and challenges, yet we have never given up on each other despite all of our flaws and imperfections. My life would not be the same without you I am "Perfectly and completely incandescently happy"

About the Author

Heather Jones is wife to her husband, Jeremy, and mother to 6 children. Driven by her entrepreneurial spirit, she worked hard to create a successful business. She soon became known for her talent as a professional hair and makeup artist and sought perfection with herself and her work. Over the years she recognized that even the most beautiful supermodels struggled with issues of self-worth and low self-esteem. She came to realize that beauty truly is only skin deep.

While struggling with the loss of her infant son, Calvin, her inner turmoil became almost unbearable. Weighed down with the heaviness of her life and heartache, through divine intervention, she was introduced to new, powerful ways of healing that brought her great inner peace.

Amazed at the speed and depth of her healing, she eagerly began her studies of several alternative healing modalities. Over the next five years, Heather trained as a Certified Reiki Master, NLP Coach, and learned all she could about Emotion Code, Inner Wise, and Hypnotherapy.

Through her studies and devotion to seek personal development, she found even greater peace and healing in her own life and made it her mission to help others do the same.

She wanted to show others that it was possible for them to overcome their own emotional traumas and limiting beliefs and that they could transform their lives. She now uses her voice to help others discover that they have a divine worth and unlimited potential. For more information visit her website at www.todaysheis.com